CRYPTOCURRENCY INVESTING

The Ultimate Guide to Investing in Bitcoin, Ethereum and Blockchain Technology

by

Devan Hansel

© 2017 Devan Hansel

All rights reserved. No part of this book may be reproduced in any form without permission in writing from the author. Reviewers may quote brief passages in their reviews.

Disclaimer

No part of this publication may be reproduced or transmitted in any form or by any means, mechanical or electronic, including photocopying or recording, or by any information storage and retrieval system, or transmitted by email without permission in writing from the publisher.

While all attempts have been made to verify the information provided in this publication, neither the author nor the publisher assumes any responsibility for errors, omissions, or contrary interpretations of the subject matter herein.

This book is for entertainment purposes only. The views expressed are those of the author alone, and should not be taken as expert instruction or commands. The reader is responsible for his or her own actions.

Adherence to all applicable laws and regulations, including international, federal, state, and local governing professional licensing, business practices, advertising, and all other aspects of doing business in the US, Canada, or any other jurisdiction is the sole responsibility of the purchaser or reader.

Neither the author nor the publisher assumes any responsibility or liability whatsoever on the behalf of the purchaser or reader of these materials.

Any perceived slight of any individual or organization is purely unintentional.

Get the FREE Bonus NOW!

If you're interested in receiving free PDFs on latest strategies, guides and secret tips about topics like cryptocurrency, bitcoin, blockchain, online trading, investing, real estate, stock market etc., I highly recommend you to join my list (link below) I've spent many years understanding all this stuff and I will provide you the distilled knowledge that can not only save you hundreds of hours but also thousands of dollars. Members in my list essentially get to learn how to make money and invest it wisely. To Subscribe, go to the link below.

www.bit.ly/devan-hansel

As a bonus, members will also be getting my latest books for FREE before anyone else. Yes, FREE. However, this is an exclusive invite and will expire soon. It doesn't cost you anything to join. You will only have to put in your email-id so that I can connect with you and keep you updated. It's a clear win-win. So, go ahead and subscribe now by visiting the previous link.

Note to the Readers

First off, I'd like to commend you for actually following up on your curiosity and getting this book. Given the public interest and rising market valuation of cryptocurrencies, this book is definitely a smart and timely purchase. The value of cryptocurrencies has skyrocketed since their inception back in 2009 with Bitcoin. A window of opportunity has opened up for those who are interested enough to learn and brave enough to invest. Make no mistake, there is a lot of wealth to be made in this field. 2 years from now, people will look back and wonder why they didn't get on the boat while they still had the chance. The fact that you've bought this book indicates your interest. But are you willing to seize the opportunity?

A lot of time and effort has gone into creating the book you are now reading. And I sincerely hope that it helps you move ahead in your quest for useful knowledge. The book has been designed to take you gradually through the hoops and introduce the cryptocurrency investing landscape, one block at a time. As such, care has been taken to ensure that anybody can read and understand the material without too many prerequisites. The book has also been written in a short-and-concise format to allow readers to flip through the book quickly. However, if you happen to find it difficult at times, please go through the resources recommended within the context. Good Luck!

About the Author

Hi there! I am Devan Hansel. I'm a crypto-investor and cat lover. Over the years, I've acquired a wide range of experiences in investing and the art of money-making. I've been involved in the stock market, real estate, tech startups and more recently...cryptocurrencies and blockchain. Having studied computer science and finance in college, I could easily grasp the essence of the technology and understand how the whole system works. In this book, I've laid out all the essential knowledge you need to understand to start tapping the market and make profitable investments quickly. I've put my maximum effort in making it interesting and understandable. I hope you have a good time reading the book :)

Come join my list if you want to follow latest trends in the marketplace and get huge discounts on early releases of my books. All you need to do is enter your email-id in the link below so that I can communicate with you about my latest works and keep you in the loop.

www.bit.ly/devan-hansel

Table of Contents

WHY YOU SHOULD READ THIS BOOK............................ 11

INTRODUCTION TO CRYPTOCURRENCY INVESTING 16

CHATPER-1: OVERVIEW OF CRYPTOCURRENCY 20

CHATPER-2: THE BLOCKCHAIN ECOSYSTEM 35

CHATPER-3: BASICS OF CRYPTOCURRENCY INVESTING 68

CHAPTER-4: YOUR FIRST CRYPTO INVESTMENT 97

CHATPER-5: HOW TO CONDUCT MARKET RESEARCH 110

CHATPER-6: ESSENTIAL TIPS & STRATEGIES 124

CHATPER-7: HOW TO PROFIT FROM ICOS 137

CHATPER-8: FUTURE OF CRYPTOCURRENCIES 145

A FEW FINAL WORDS 156

MORE FROM THE AUTHOR 157

Why You Should Read This Book

If you're interested in capturing wealth then the cryptocurrency market is undoubtedly the #1 place to go to right now. Millionaires are being made in a matter of months. This is a fact. You can check out any worthy blog or newspaper or YouTube channel to understand this. There are many Bitcoin millionaires who have received a whopping 3000% return on their investments. With basic knowledge of the underlying technology and some market research, anybody can make sensible bets and reap the profits.

You might be wondering if the market has faded out and if there really is as much opportunity now as there was 2 or 3 years back. If you are, let me make it clear to you. 1 Bitcoin was worth around $19,000 by end of 2017. Experts predict that it will reach a whopping $100,000 (or even more) in only 5 years. This is not a wild guess. It is a well analyzed forecast from the top experts in cryptocurrency. So, 5 years from now, you could be sitting on **massive profits** or you could look back and regret for not having taken a calculated risk. To help you decide, let me elaborate more. Listed below are the factors that make cryptocurrency investing a sensible option.

- **Cryptocurrencies are decentralized**. That means, no single financial organization or hedge fund can control the stock value or use market manipulation tricks. The power is with the public. And the technology that supports this open decentralized framework is called Blockchain which will be covered in chapter-2.

2. **The market is super young.** The first cryptocurrency, Bitcoin, was released in 2009 and trading cryptocurrencies picked up steam around 2012-2013. So, it's only around 5-6 years old. Very small percent of the global population is even aware of cryptocurrencies and even smaller percent knows how to make profits from them. So, the chances for capturing a piece of the pie are extremely high.

3. **Network effect.** The success of a currency depends on how many people use it and how well it's able to handle transactions. As more people adapt cryptocurrencies, it will speed up the pace of adaption and even more people will learn about them and adapt them. That's the

beauty of network effects. If you get paid only in Bitcoins, companies that want you as a customer will be forced to accept your Bitcoins.

Hopefully after reading this, you've understood why exactly it's a gold mine right now. The next steps are to equip you with a shovel and teach you how to dig the gold, metaphorically speaking. Chapters 1 & 2 will teach you the fundamentals of cryptocurrency technology. If you're in a hurry or are already familiar with the details, you can skip chapter-2 which deals with the blockchain technology and why it works the way it does. Chapter-3 talks about the basic terminology and explains essential concepts like cryptoexchange, wallet etc. In chapter-4, you will make your first investment to test the market. Chapters 5,6,7 will teach you about the strategies you can use to pick profitable investments and avoid unnecessary pitfalls. And the final chapter will help you understand where the cryptocurrency market is headed in the near future. So, without further ado, let's get started.

Introduction to Cryptocurrency Investing

Nowadays, words like 'cryptocurrency', 'bitcoin', 'blockchain' are being used all around us. They are talked about in board meetings, tech events, major blogs, publications and news channels. But what exactly is all this about? Why are so many billionaires, Silicon Valley icons and financial authorities calling this the next technological and financial revolution? We will learn the answer to this in the upcoming chapters. If you're not familiar with any of the terms or if you're a beginner who is interested in getting a deeper look at this latest phenomenon, you're at the right place...and at the right time too. From the basics of cryptocurrencies to detailed strategies on profiting from the current market trends, you are about to experience the essence of the subject in an entertaining and educational manner. Brace yourself!

So, what exactly are cryptocurrencies?

To put it short, cryptocurrencies are virtual currencies that use mathematical operations to carry out transactions. They have certain properties like decentralization, durability etc. (we will cover these in later chapters). So, almost everything about cryptocurrencies is digitized including the currency units, regulatory limits, security etc. Individual units of cryptocurrency are referred to as "crypto coins" or "coins". You can buy a certain number of coins and hold it in your digital wallet or "crypto wallet". The most famous cryptocurrency is Bitcoin which is also the first that was released publicly. Although it's a relatively recent invention, the market scope and investments have grown exponentially. In fact, the current market cap for all tradeable cryptocurrencies is around $584 Billion!

What is Cryptocurrency Investing?

Cryptocurrency Investing or CryptoInvesting for short, is a process of putting your funds into a cryptocurrency platform and purchasing the coins so as to have their value increase over time. The most significant reason for cryptoinvesting is to make huge returns. The basic elements of cryptoinvesting are: an entry strategy, a portfolio management strategy and an exit strategy. We will cover all of these in depth in upcoming chapters.

Chatper-1: Overview of Cryptocurrency

Before we dive into the nitty-gritty details of cryptocurrency investing, it is important to first understand exactly how they work. Terms like *blockchain*, *mining*, *cryptowallet* will appear frequently in later chapters. You will also need to be equipped with basic knowledge of cryptocurrency ecosystem before you can start day trading or investing in any of the available options. So, let's begin. We will start with the basics and slowly proceed to advanced concepts, tips and strategies.

The Origin of Cryptocurrency

Throughout history, we've used different mediums of exchange like commodity money, paper money, gold standard, fiat currencies etc. But over the years, different scientific communities across the world had been dissatisfied with the short-comings of these traditional currencies. Due to the explosion of internet and progress made in the fields of cryptography, online security, digital payments, it became possible to have a totally decentralized currency that could void the necessity of a central bank or government.

After the 9/11 attacks, America got very strict on the digital front. Laws like the *Patriot Act* were passed to perform online surveillance at a mass level. Needless to say, cryptocurrencies were shunned down owing to their decentralized structure and assumed to be hotbeds for terrorists and other illegal activities.

The first sign of cryptocurrency came when an American cryptographer named David Chaum founded the company *DigiCash* in Netherlands (since it was likely to get shut down in America). DigiCash used *blinding algorithms* to protect user's money and transaction details. However, they had complete monopoly over the supply of the currency and they dealt with the users directly. This made the Central Bank of Netherlands call foul which meant that DigiCash would have to either sell the company or shut it down soon. Although Microsoft approached DigiCash with an offer of $180 million, Chaum thought that it was not enough. So, Microsoft took the offer off the table and DigiCash ran out of funds eventually.

Shortly after that, many cryptocurrency systems like *b-money* and *BitGold* came into light but never took off. They had all the necessary components like blockchain systems, anonymity protection, decentralization etc. but somehow couldn't get enough attention in the marketplace for widespread usage.

The first modern cryptocurrency to emerge that is effective and used widely is Bitcoin. A white-paper explaining the details of bitcoin implementation was first published under the pseudo-name of *Satoshi Nakamoto* in October 2008. The paper is titled "*Bitcoin: A Peer-to-Peer Electronic Cash System*" and can be downloaded at www.bitcoin.org/bitcoin.pdf. On January 2009, Satoshi released the initial version of the bitcoin software on SourceForge.net, opening the technology up to the public. To this day, the real identity of Satoshi Nakomoto remains a mystery. Based on bitcoin transaction logs, it is estimated that Satoshi owns roughly 1 million bitcoins which are currently evaluated at around 17 billion dollars!

Cryptocurrencies are slowly being accepted by all major companies and startups, especially in Silicon Valley. WordPress became the first major company to accept bitcoins in 2012. Soon after, big shots like Microsoft, Tesla, Dell, Virgin Group, Lamborghini followed. Currently, the total market cap for all cryptocurrencies has exceeded $630 billion. This is an indication that the world is slowly shifting towards decentralized cryptocurrencies for a myriad of reasons.

Different types of cryptocurrencies

More than 1000 public cryptocurrencies exist in the world and many more are created every month. In this section, we will look at the most prominent cryptocurrencies. To view the updated trends and market capitalizations of the top 100 cryptocurrencies, check out CoinMarketCap (www.coinmarketcap.com).

1. **Bitcoin (BTC):** This is the first known cryptocurrency that is well recognized and used by the public. It has paved the way for modern cryptocurrencies and is considered to be the de facto standard. Almost all the other cryptocurrencies have either branched off from or have major commonalities with bitcoin. Market cap of bitcoin stands at around 270 billion dollars by the end of 2017 making it the largest publicly traded digital currency. For a detailed guide on how Bitcoin works and how to properly invest in it, check out my book "*Bitcoin: The Digital Gold*" on Amazon.

2. **Litecoin (LTC)**: Launched around 2 years after bitcoin, litecoin is a decentralized peer-to-peer

cryptocurrency with a growing network of developers, merchants and supporters. Although very similar to bitcoin, it offers relatively faster transaction confirmations. Where bitcoin is gold, litecoin is silver.

3. **Ethereum(ETH)**: Launched recently (2015), ethereum is also a decentralized cryptocurrency but offers more functionality like *smart contracts*, the *ethereum virtual machine*, distributed computing etc. As of Jan 2018, Ethereum is the second largest cryptocurrency with a market cap of around 100 billion dollars.

4. **Ripple (XRP)**: Ripple is heavily used by banks to settle global transactions in a secure and effective way at very low costs. It is different from bitcoin

in its protocol and structure. Unlike bitcoin, ripple doesn't require high computing power for creation of new currency. As a result, it has a reduced network latency. The individual units of Ripple currency are called *ripples* (XRP). At the time of this writing, Ripple has a market capitalization of 48 billion dollars making it the third largest cryptocurrency.

5. **Dash (DASH)**: Originally known as DarkCoin, Dash is also a decentralized peer-to-peer cryptocurrency like Bitcoin albeit a more secretive one. It was launched in January 2014 and experienced a surge in traffic and fan-following quickly. Its famous features include instant transactions (*InstantSend*) and complete private transactions (*PrivateSend*). It also uses a

separate chained hashing algorithm called X11 unlike bitcoin's SHA256.

Note: Cryptocurrencies other than Bitcoin are referred to as "Altcoins" because they are alternatives launched after Bitcoin.

Bitcoin

As you must've already understood by now, the most promising and widely used cryptocurrency is Bitcoin. So, let's look at the factors that make Bitcoin such an awesome currency and why it's a no-brainer to invest in it. For a deep-dive into Bitcoin and how you can potentially make thousands of dollars mining and trading bitcoins, check out my book "*Bitcoin: The Digital Gold*" on Amazon.

Why Bitcoin is a good currency

1. **Scarcity**: Only 21 million bitcoins can ever exist. We will see why in further chapters. This cap on the total number of bitcoins ensures that its net value never drops too low. As the economy grows, the value of bitcoin also increases. It is estimated that one bitcoin will be worth around 1 million dollars in less than 10 years. And it costs less than $20,000 by the end of 2017. (If you're planning to purchase and invest in bitcoins, check out Chapter-5)

2. **Durability**: The whole purpose of currency is to represent money in a physical/virtual form so that people can have easier time exchanging value. If the currency fades away with time or gets worn out over repeated use, it can be a hassle to keep churning out more currency to replace the damage. All physical currencies are prone to physical damage like wear & tear, weather etc. This is where bitcoin trumps all other forms of currencies because it is 100% digital. The life-time of a bitcoin is theoretically infinite. It will survive as long as there's an operating network that runs the bitcoin protocol. A decentralized network, high level of encryption, digitized currency and the existential guarantee of internet in the foreseeable future make bitcoin

one of the most durable currencies ever created.

3. **Interchangeable**: We already know that currency is just a set of monetary units in use. As such, a good currency is one in which the units are interchangeable. This means that all the units should be identical in *structure* and represent the same amount of value. Take gold for example. 1 gram of gold has the same value anywhere. Similarly, 1 bitcoin is exactly the same as the other. For all practical purposes, you can exchange 1 bitcoin with another and there would be no difference in value.

4. **Divisibility**: To measure and grade value, a good currency needs to be divisible to the smallest required scale (e.g., dollars & cents,

pounds & pence, rupees & paisa). The bitcoin protocol has been designed in such a way that you can divide one bitcoin into many smaller units called Satoshis which can be further divided if necessary.

5. **Transferability**: If you have a working internet connection and a computer (smartphone or tablet will also work), you can transfer bitcoins with just a couple of clicks. This makes it a very convenient mode of money transfer unlike bank cheques and wire transfers. There is no central authority or third party that charges a transfer fee so it is also a more profitable mode of money transfer.

Now that you know what makes Bitcoin a good currency, the next step is to register for a CoinBase account and try buying some Bitcoin. CoinBase is a platform for buying and selling cryptocurrency. It is one of the best options available in the market. I use it myself for all kinds of cryptocurrency related activities and would highly recommend it to you as well. Go to the link below to sign up and get $10 of FREE Bitcoin for your future trades.

www.coinbase.com/join/598b36cb68284c0125fa0aea

Chatper-2: The Blockchain Ecosystem

In this chapter, we will look at the foundation on which most cryptocurrencies rely on – the blockchain. If you're a beginner to this technology, make sure to take your time while going through the different sections. It is going to get a bit technical. Reference links have been provided where necessary for better understanding. If you're more interested in the trading part, you may choose to skip this chapter and proceed to chapter-3.

What is Blockchain?

Let us begin by asking the question – what do we need a currency for? We need currency so that we can give it to others (buying) or take it from others (selling). Isn't this true? And for a cryptocurrency, that is where a blockchain comes into the picture. Blockchain is a technology that allows people to transfer cryptocurrency between one another securely. It is a distributed database where all the transaction records are saved. Unlike a typical fiat currency like USD, the blockchain of cryptocurrency is distributed and spread across various countries and individuals. The databases and servers are run by volunteers who maintain a peer-to-peer network. There is no possibility of government or any third-party involvement in manipulating the database records. Even if the government officials or any malicious entities volunteer for maintaining the blockchain, they cannot alter the transaction records due to the constraints imposed by its design.

Blockchain is essentially an open electronic ledger where all transactions are recorded for public viewing. These transactions are grouped together into blocks. And as the name suggests, the blockchain is essentially a chain of valid blocks. For example, all the latest bitcoin transactions can be found at: www.blockchain.info. This open strategy of blockchain prevents counterfeits and other frauds. By checking the blockchain, you can be sure that the transactions are completely legitimate. Once you make a transaction, it will appear shortly in the public blockchain.

You might be wondering, *"But won't people know who's spending how much by looking at the blockchain?"*. The answer to that is *No* because your identity is protected using encryption and mapping functions. Only your Wallet-ID will appear in the blockchain which reveals nothing about your personal identity. We will cover the mechanics of a cryptocurrency wallet in the next chapter.

What is Mining?

Now that we have an idea of what the blockchain is, it is necessary to understand how it is updated unanimously throughout the network. It has to be unanimous because if the status of blockchain is not congruent among the nodes, it will lead to discrepancies in verifying transactions which will result in frauds and eventual system failure. So, let's look into this in detail.

There are two kinds of nodes in a blockchain network. Normal nodes and mining nodes. Both of these have their own separate operating protocols. And every node maintains its own blockchain, constructed individually by adding valid blocks to the list. The normal nodes have relatively basic functionality. They receive transaction-messages from neighboring nodes in the network and their job is to verify the transactions and propagate them forward to remaining nodes. This will ensure that as time goes by, only verified transactions are spread across the network. This is a basic layer of security to ensure bogus transactions are not updated in the blockchain.

Now, the mining nodes are a different kind of nodes that execute the *mining protocol* which includes the following steps.

→ Listen for new transactions and verify them.

→ Aggregate verified transactions into a block.

→ Compute the solution to an algorithm called *Proof-of-Work* for that specific block.

→ Timestamp the block along with the computed *proof-of-work solution* and broadcast it across the network.

The mining nodes essentially group new valid transactions into blocks and propagate them to other nodes. The validity of the block can be measured by any node by checking the *proof-of-work* value. So, when this new block is received by the remaining nodes, they check its validity and add it to their own blockchain. A reward is given to the mining node that propagated the valid block with the earliest timestamp. This reward is usually a certain amount of cryptocurrency units. It is similar to the processing fee charged by banks and other financial organizations. Once a block is verified and added to the blockchain, it is said to have been successfully mined.

Now we know how blocks are mined, how the blockchain is built and how the *Proof-of-Work* protocol helps in making sure that every node on the network is on the same page when it comes to the blockchain. Here's the interesting part. In most cryptocurrencies (including Bitcoin), mining is the only way to create new crypto-coins. That is to say, the only way for the system to assign value to the cryptocurrency is to measure the amount of computation performed by the mining nodes. Every bitcoin ever mined has been the result of a mining node performing the *Proof-of-Work* algorithm to create a new valid block.

So, the purpose of mining is twofold. To create new cryptocurrency and update the blockchain with valid transactions. The reason that miners are rewarded is to incentivize them to perform the needed computation. If there was no reward, there wouldn't be enough miners to validate the transactions quickly. This would lead to high latency in the network which would make the whole system rather unsafe. The security of the cryptocurrency depends on how fast the transactions are verified. And that depends on how many miners are competing for the reward simultaneously. This is the beauty of the bitcoin-blockchain system design. And also, the reward for mining goes down by 50% every 4 years for the bitcoin system. Eventually, there would be no reward for mining blocks except for the transaction fee and tips. This is a way to limit the supply of the cryptocurrency and ensure its value doesn't go down below a certain threshold.

The Blockchain is the heart of most cryptocurrencies. It is the bedrock on which all the transactions, security and efficiency of the system rely upon. Moreover, the tech community across the globe is waking up to the ingenuity of the blockchain design. Numerous applications of the blockchain technology are being identified in all areas of the digital spectrum. It may as well be that we've stumbled upon the backbone of a new kind of internet. If you're really interested in learning more about this to get a complete perspective, check out my book *"Blockchain: The Technology Revolution behind Bitcoin and Cryptocurrency"*.

The two main problems that a blockchain solves are:

1. Decentralized Consensus
2. Double Spending

How Decentralized Consensus Works

The architecture of the blockchain is such that it eliminates the need for a central database or monitoring authority. You have to understand that this is a groundbreaking technological revolution not only in the field of digital currency but also in business, banking, governance, politics etc. A plethora of possibilities have opened up after it has been proven that a system like bitcoin can be developed which achieves decentralized consensus in a secure and efficient manner. New self-verifying systems and decentralized apps are being developed today on account of this innovation.

To those who are unaware, decentralized consensus is a scenario where a network of entities comes to a common agreement about something (in our case, the validity of a transaction) without having to trust one another. This is also known as distributed trust-less consensus and is a major research topic in the field of Distributed Systems. Many algorithms have been designed to solve this problem of distributed consensus. Cryptocurrencies like Bitcoin use a specific protocol called *Proof of Work* (POW), as we've seen, which lets the blockchain network achieve distributed consensus and operate without getting tampered with. It is important to understand why achieving distributed consensus is so important in a cryptocurrency's blockchain network.

Let's assume that you have a network of computers (or "nodes") that are interconnected in a haphazard manner. This network forms the *backend* of your service. In other words, all the computation and database storage operations are handled by this network *behind the scenes*. Your objective is to ensure that when a user performs an action, it has to be recorded and updated congruently throughout the network. So, your network is distributed but you have to project a single consistent experience to users everywhere. This is the most basic requirement for not only a cryptocurrency like bitcoin but also for almost every technology company out there like Google, Facebook, Amazon, Instagram etc.

When a user performs an action, you will observe that in order to achieve the objective of consistency, you are inevitably left with only two options. Either record this action in all the nodes or none of the nodes. If you record it in only some of the nodes, there is an inconsistency in the network and the nodes cannot figure out the truth i.e., whether the user did actually perform the action or not. In other words, the network cannot come to an agreeable consensus. This is a big problem because an inconsistent network is an insecure network. Any hacker would be able to exploit this inconsistency to spread viruses or manipulate the database to his/her advantage. Therefore, it is important for a distributed network to maintain consistent data across all nodes and be able to identify erroneous and inconsistent records quickly. This is the reason why distributed consensus is so important in a blockchain network.

Now let's look at how exactly the blockchain aids in achieving this decentralized consensus. We will be considering bitcoin as the reference cryptocurrency.

Decentralized consensus in a blockchain is truly amazing. This is because all the nodes in the network are able to agree on the validity of a transaction without having to trust anyone else or knowing the identity of parties involved. That is why it is also known as trust-less decentralized consensus.

Decentralized consensus in a cryptocurrency using blockchain is achieved in an emergent manner. What this means is that there is no single point of time at which all the nodes in the network are able to agree on the validity of a transaction. As time progresses, more and more nodes will be able to arrive at the same conclusion.

There are four phases in which this emergent distributed consensus is achieved. Let's look at them closely.

Phase #1: Verification of every incoming transaction by every node.

The nodes in the network receive data regarding various transactions from their neighboring nodes. Some of these transactions are just invalid. So, as a primary rule, all the nodes check the incoming transactions and collect the valid ones into what is called as a *transaction pool* or *mempool*. The transactions are verified using cryptographic techniques based on a list of criteria that are public.

And this pool of valid but unconfirmed transactions are propagated across the network by each node. So, all the invalid transactions are weeded out by the nodes in the network in the first phase.

Phase #2: Mining nodes accumulate valid transactions into blocks.

Mining nodes, as we've seen earlier, are special nodes in the network whose job is to collect valid transactions from their neighboring nodes, put them in a block and compute a unique value ("*Proof of Work*") for the block using a cryptographic algorithm. The mining nodes keep track of the latest blocks and compete with each other to create a new block of these valid transactions with the appropriate *proof-of-work*. These blocks are then propagated across the network to other nodes.

Phase #3: Nodes receive and verify blocks

As the nodes in the network receive blocks from various mining nodes, they calculate their validity. Anybody can accumulate transactions into blocks. But the trick here is that computing the correct *"proof-of-work"* of a block is very hard and therefore reduces the chance of a transaction fraud. Once the nodes receive a mining node's block, they verify it against the *"proof-of-work"* and add it to their blockchain which they've been maintaining and updating so far.

Phase #4: Nodes eliminate irrelevant blocks

Every node maintains and updates its own blockchain which is essentially a list of blocks that are considered valid using publicly known and accepted criteria. Nodes can receive multiple valid blocks by different mining nodes. So how can they decide collectively as to which of the received blocks should be considered while extending the blockchain? This is where the proof-of-work protocol comes in handy. Different blocks have different proof-of-work values. The bitcoin protocol states that while selecting blocks, preference should be given to the block with the highest proof-of-work value. So, if a node gets two different blocks, it will maintain two separate lists in the blockchain until one of them exceeds the other in the total cumulative proof-of-work value sum. It will then discard the sub-chain with lower proof-of-work value sum. In a way, the nodes give preference to the sub-chain in which the mining nodes have spent more computational power because the *proof-of-work* value sum is a measure of the amount of computation done by the mining nodes.

The Double-Spending Problem

The concept of blockchain was first brought to light by the Bitcoin inventor, Satoshi Nakamoto. It was (and still is) considered a brilliant engineering design partly because it was able to solve what no other digital currency could before that point of time which is to *'Ensure that the cryptocurrency units cannot be spent more than once.'* This is termed as the double spending problem.

Unlike fiat currency, the problem with a virtual currency is not the creation of the currency units. Anybody can come up with protocols/algorithms defining how the virtual currency units need to be created, how they need to be structured, what the size (in bytes) of each unit should be and so on. But the fundamental problem that any currency, especially a digital currency, needs to solve is *Double Spending*.

A *double-spend* is a scenario in which one unit of currency is spent in two separate transactions. This can be done by duplicating the unit itself or manipulating the record of transactions. In case of cryptocurrencies, this 'record' is the blockchain ledger.

A typical fiat currency solves the double-spending problem by deploying special techniques to print the cash and identify fake bills. The banks that deal with fiat currency transactions also take extensive security measures to prevent their databases (which hold all the transaction and account details) from getting hacked and hijacked. If the security of the bank's computer-network was compromised, the potential for damage is huge. With countless cases of bank frauds, hacking attacks and duplication of cash, it is evident that a fiat currency's solution to the double-spending problem is undoubtedly flawed.

So, how does a cryptocurrency like bitcoin solve this?

Unlike a centralized fiat currency, a system like bitcoin does not maintain "balances" of the individuals. It only maintains a ledger of transactions a.k.a the blockchain. So, the only way to handle this issue is by assigning identifiers to bitcoins so that when someone tries to spend a bitcoin with the same identifier twice, it can be checked against the transactions recorded in the blockchain.

The way this works is, whenever you send someone bitcoins, that transaction is identified and recorded using a UTXO which is short for Unspent Transaction Output. This UTXO is the unique identifier that represents a transaction of bitcoins which is similar to a bill of fiat currency. UTXOs can be spent only as wholes. But they can be converted into multiple smaller UTXOs for transaction convenience.

When you want to spend some bitcoins, you have to either merge or split two UTXOs to create the new set of UTXOs you want. For example, assume that you have two UTXOs of 0.3 and 0.6 bitcoins, received from Alice and Bob respectively. Let's refer to these using their IDs, X and Y. So, X represents the UTXO of Alice and Y that of Bob. And let's say that you want to send 0.7 bitcoins to Carter. The conversion goes as follows:

X (0.3 bitcoins) + Y (0.6 bitcoins) => Z (0.7 bitcoins) + W (0.2 bitcoins)

Z and W represent the unique IDs of two new UTXOs created so that 0.7 bitcoins can be sent to Carter. Now, this new UTXO (Z) can only be spent when used in conjunction with Carter's signature. It is propagated across the network and eventually picked up by a mining node which hashes it into a block and updates the blockchain. That is how the transaction takes place. And the conversion is handled by a software called the *cryptocurrency wallet* which we'll be looking into in the next chapter. The other UTXO (W) worth 0.2 bitcoins goes back into your wallet and is spendable only in conjunction with your signature.

With this framework in place, all that a node has to do to verify if a bitcoin is being "double-spent" is to check the UTXO ID against the blockchain's transactions. Even if a node's blockchain is incomplete, the faulty UTXO will get propagated only so far before getting dropped by the other nodes with complete blockchain which can verify latest transactions.

Who maintains the servers and Why?

You must be wondering, if maintaining and updating the blockchain takes so much effort, who would want to do this? Why would anyone want to volunteer for this kind of a task?

The answer to that is *Mining incentives.* As we've already seen, most cryptocurrencies are designed in such a way that the people who validate transactions and update the blockchain are rewarded with new crypto-coins. This serves as an incentive for their efforts. Rewarding the miners is the only sustainable way of maintaining a distributed decentralized cryptocurrency network. This is because mining the crypto-coins requires a lot of computational power provided by specialized GPUs and also involves paying a lot of money in electricity bill.

It also happens to be that mining is the only way of generating cryptocurrency i.e., the new crypto-coins in the network are only generated when a miner creates a new valid block. This is a clever strategy to solve two problems in one shot. The miners get incentivized and the network gets new crypto-coins to work with.

It is very important for the system to be designed in such a way that **anybody** can come in and volunteer as a miner in the network. If the ability to mine was exclusive, the banks or the government or the top 1% could find a way to attain too much control over the system. This could jeopardize the safety and decentralization of the cryptocurrency. For example, if a bank was bombed and/or it's servers were hacked, it's customers would be in trouble. But with a widespread network of mining volunteers, there wouldn't be a single point of failure. This was something that Satoshi Nakomoto made sure of, while designing the system framework.

Why is it safe?

For the purpose of answering this question, let's narrow our focus down to one single cryptocurrency – bitcoin. Bitcoin is the most widely used cryptocurrency in the world. Millions of people pay close attention to the bitcoin network every day. The software itself undergoes regular public updates. A 2013 article on Forbes suggests that the global bitcoin computing power is 256 times more than the top 500 supercomputers in the world. That should give you a measure of the number of servers being run by the bitcoin volunteers. So, at this point of time, the only possible ways to hack bitcoin are either taking down the internet or cracking the SHA256 function. SHA256 is one of the most famous security functions used in the Bitcoin protocol to encrypt data into output of 256-bits (32 bytes) size. It is deemed to be uncrackable. This of course, is regarding the overall bitcoin network and the system design. You can still get your bitcoins lost/stolen if you do not follow the recommended security measures (described in the next chapter) while operating your wallet.

Although cracking the SHA256 algorithm is next to impossible, it is important to understand the difference between safety and anonymity in the context of cryptocurrencies. The fact that SHA256 is hard to crack only implies that an attack on the blockchain or stealing your crypto-coins is extremely unlikely. It, however, does not mean that you are anonymous within the system. This is one of the biggest misconceptions about bitcoin and other cryptocurrencies. Your bitcoins are safe but your identity is not a total secret.

Most cryptocurrencies including Bitcoin only provide pseudonymity and not complete anonymity. Although your identity is not revealed openly, the transaction details are updated on the blockchain which is accessible by anyone. Using techniques like cluster analysis and pattern recognition on the data from the public blockchain, one can start to form associations with your activity and your IP-address (which is essentially your online identity). Now, you can use software like Tor or VPN to hide your IP address but the fact of the matter is that even Tor cannot guarantee complete anonymity. A dedicated hacker with enough resources can eventually track your IP address down. But, he/she will not be able to steal or tamper with your crypto-coins as long as you follow the proper security measures and store your crypto-coins in a safe wallet. Having said that, if you're still concerned, I would recommend that you choose Zcash as it is the most pseudonymous cryptocurrency out there.

Chatper-3: Basics of Cryptocurrency Investing

There is a lot of euphoria in the crypto market currently. And that calls for caution. As Warren Buffet said, *"Be fearful when others are greedy and greedy when others are fearful."* And the recent upsurge in the valuation of cryptocurrencies indicates a lot of greed in the market currently. People are buying in like crazy and many are holding on to what they've got. There is a lot of hype going around. This is the time for caution and paying careful attention to the market while getting educated on the subject. And that's what we're going to do. In the next few sections, we will look at all the basics of crypto-investing and understand terminology like crypto-wallet, crypto-exchange etc. We will also be looking at some of the top cryptocurrencies available in the market and what they have to offer.

How to store cryptocurrencies

For regular fiat currencies, we all know where to store them i.e., in banks and wallets (online/offline). But how do you store cryptocurrencies? And how do you ensure that they're safe from thefts and attacks? We will look at how these problems are handled by a software called the "wallet" in the next section.

Cryptocurrency wallet

A cryptocurrency wallet, or *crypto-wallet* for short, is a digital holder for your cryptocurrency (like bitcoin) and is mandatory for performing transactions. It stores your private, public keys and manages your cryptocurrency transactions by interacting with the blockchain. There is no such thing as a bitcoin without a wallet identification. Every cryptocurrency unit has to be associated with, and transacted using, a wallet. You cannot spend your crypto-coins without the wallet. You also cannot spend the same crypto-coins from multiple wallets because it doesn't tally with the blockchain's record.

There are different types of wallets you can use. You will find next, an image of a mobile wallet which is essentially a mobile app that stores your public & private key data and manages your transactions. The specific screenshot has been taken from the *Bitcoin Wallet* app on Google Play Store. There are other types of wallet frameworks like desktop wallet application, online wallet(website), hardware wallet (USB drive, hard disk etc.), paper wallet (printed sheet of keys in a QR code).

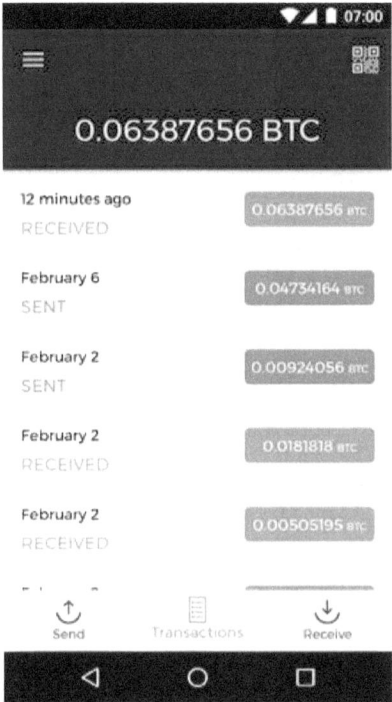

How does the wallet work?

A cryptowallet holds 3 primary values. The public key, private key and the amount of crypto-coins. As we've seen, the primary purpose of a wallet is to facilitate cryptocurrency transactions. Here's how it does it.

Let's say that you want to send bitcoins to your friend. Your wallet will generate the transaction-message, number of bitcoins you want to send and sign it with your private key and your friend's public key. This message is then communicated over an online network channel with your friend on it. Your friend's wallet will verify if the message is in fact sent by you and intended for him by decrypting it with his private key and your public key.

After the authenticity is established and the possibility of a middle-man is eliminated, your friend's wallet increases the number of bitcoins it holds and sends a response. Once your wallet receives the response, it decreases your bitcoin amount.

There is a specific Wallet protocol put in place to ensure that the amounts in the two wallets corresponding to a transaction are modified correctly. Anybody who wishes to implement their own wallet software must adhere to this protocol or else the transactions won't be processed.

After the amounts in both the wallets are modified, the blockchain is updated with the transaction entry. It takes some time for the blockchain network to validate the transaction. If all goes well, the ledger moves forward otherwise the error in the system will notify the wallets and the change is reverted. This concludes a typical wallet use-case scenario.

For the purpose of simplicity, many details have been omitted. If you're looking for more specifics, please visit the official bitcoin developer guide on this topic.

Security Measures for Wallets

Losing the wallet or the keys will result in ***TOTAL LOSS*** of your cryptocurrency. It might helpful to learn about a famous real-life story of James Howells who lost 7500 bitcoins (worth around $120 million today) because he accidentally threw his old hard drive into the trash bin while clearing his desk. That hard drive is now reportedly buried under four feet of junk in a landfill site in Newport. So, make no mistake, the security of your wallet should be your top most priority when dealing with cryptocurrency. Here are some tips to follow.

Tip #1: There are different wallet software you can choose for any cryptocurrency. Please use only an officially recognized wallet to avoid issues of security and malfunction. Take some time and go through the wallet specifications and your cryptocurrency's website to pick what's best. For bitcoin, you can find all the recommended bitcoin wallets at the link below.

www.bitcoin.org/en/choose-your-wallet.

Tip #2: Encrypt your wallet and private key and have multiple copies stored in secure locations (online and offline). Make sure that you have at least one copy available in an accessible physical device like a flash drive or a hard disk.

Tip #3: If the amount of your cryptocurrency is substantial, it is recommended to use multiple wallets to distribute the coins and reduce the possible damage that can happen. Use 2-step verification methods or MultiSig (Multiple Signature) transactions.

Cryptocurrency Exchanges

Also called *crypto-exchanges*, these are online platforms for buying and selling cryptocurrencies.

You need to connect your wallet with a crypto-exchange to start trading or investing. You can also "buy-in" with your fiat currency after verifying your identity i.e. you can purchase BTC for, let's say, USD.

Just like regular company stocks can be traded at stock exchanges like NASDAQ, NYSE etc., cryptocurrencies can be traded at these crypto-exchanges. For a list of the top crypto exchanges, check out CryptoCoinCharts at the link below.
www.cryptocoincharts.info/markets/info

Please note that it's not necessary for an exchange to support all cryptocurrencies. And some of them might not be supported in your geographical area. So, browse through the exchanges carefully and select one that you find suitable. Here are some parameters to judge the exchange on: reputation and public opinion, supported payment options, transaction fee, geographical limitations, supported cryptocurrencies, ease of usage etc. (we will cover these shortly). The most popular exchanges are GDAX, Poloniex and Kraken.

I personally use GDAX (link below) because it satisfies all the essential criteria and offers a top-notch customer service. And so far, it has been a safe and smooth ride without any issue. It is also integrated with the Coinbase wallet so you don't need two separate accounts for managing both. I highly recommend it to beginners and anybody interested in cryptocurrency investing who wants a pleasant experience. Use the link mentioned below to sign up and get $10 bonus for your first trade.

http://www.coinbase.com/join/598b36cb68284c0125fa0aea

After picking a suitable exchange, you will need to verify your identity (via passport, driver's license etc.) to create an account. Once the account is created, you will be able to add/withdraw funds and start trading. Just like any other trading platform, you will be charged a very small fee for every trade to keep the exchange going.

You might be wondering as to why your ID is required when after all, cryptocurrencies are supposed to be decentralized and to support users' privacy/anonymity preferences. Well, here's the thing. Although the transactions themselves are private, the cryptocurrency exchange needs initial fiat currency to assign you crypto-coins to trade with. And where there is fiat currency involved, there is a non-zero probability of financial fraud. So, to avoid issues with unoriginal fiat currency (stolen credit cards etc.), the exchange does require your personal information to validate your fiat money. Once you've been verified, you can trade on the platform with privacy.

There are a few types of crypto exchanges that exist out there. So, it might help you to be aware of them before getting your feet wet.

1. **Traditional Crypto-Exchanges**: Similar to the old-school stock exchanges, these act as the "middle man" for traders looking to buy/sell cryptocurrencies at market price. A slight fee is charged for every transaction to keep the exchange going. They also let users "buy in" with regular fiat currencies. Popular examples are: GDAX, Kraken, Shapeshift.

2. **Direct Trading Exchanges**: These are a kind of "unofficial" platforms where the trade doesn't happen at the fixed market price. Instead, sellers can set their own price and trade directly with buyers. Also referred to sometimes as peer-to-peer exchanges.

3. **Crypto Brokers**: These are independent platforms that offer cryptocurrency trading, customer support, development and other services. Similar to the currency exchange booths at airports. Designed for a smooth trading experience, they provide trust and support to intermediate and advanced traders who find the traditional exchanges lacking in proper user interface and/or functionality. A good example for this is Coinbase.

Hey there! Just a quick break before we continue learning further. Let me ask you this – How do you feel? Are you already familiar with the concepts described here? Or are you enjoying learning about these new ideas and methods? Please let me know. I want you to write a review on Amazon by going to the link below. It will take no more than 2 minutes and would mean a lot to me. Thank you.

www.bookstuff.in/cryptoinvesting-review

Now let's look at the factors to consider before selecting a cryptocurrency exchange. This is an important part of the investing process since you will be holding your crypto-coins on the exchange, sometimes for long periods of time. It's better to be safe than sorry. With that, let's dig into what exactly makes a good crypto-exchange and how to check if it suits your investing needs and preferences.

- **<u>Credibility</u>**: Do your research before selecting an exchange. When you find something that looks good, ask around and investigate a little. There are a lot of good forums that can assist you like BitcoinTalk (www.bitcointalk.org), CryptoCompare (www.cryptocompare.com), Reddit (www.reddit.com/r/CryptoMarkets) etc. You can also check out the latest Google News articles, Quora answers and do a general web search to get an idea of the exchange's trustworthiness.

- **Payment method**: Does the cryptoexchange accept your preferred method of payment? Are other options like PayPal, credit/debit cards, wire transfer also accepted in case you want to change your mode of payment? On a side note, cryptoexchanges usually charge an additional premium for credit cards due to the added risk and processing fee.

- **Identity Verification**: This is a sort of protection mechanism for the exchanges to prevent users from investing black money and other frauds. But always be careful when submitting your personal information to the exchange. Uploading a government-issued public ID like Driver's license or Passport should be fine.
- **Fees Structure**: This is something that changes with every cryptoexchange. You are usually charged for either deposit, withdrawal or transactions. Exchange rate is also something that influences your investments especially when done in large amounts. The exact percentages vary widely

so you should always check the cryptoexchange's website for complete details.

- **Geographical Restrictions**: This is again one of the factors that changes a lot between exchanges. You should check if the exchange offers *full* set of features and services in your country. Also, if you plan to do investing while on vacation in another country, you should check that as well.

Now that we are well versed in the methodology behind investing like how cryptocurrencies are stored, how exchanges work, what to look at while picking an exchange etc., let's understand at a fundamental level, the answer to the following question.

Where do cryptocurrencies get value from?

One of the original reasons cryptocurrencies were invented is to store digital assets securely and avoid interference from central powers like the governments and banks. Some cryptocurrencies are backed by gold and precious metals while others have no backing except the widespread acceptance by users. So, if there is no backing from the governments and everything is distributed globally, where do cryptocurrencies actually get value from and what are the factors influencing it?

1. **Supply and Demand**: One of most popular economic principles is the correlation of price of

an object with its supply & demand. Let's take Bitcoin for example. As we've already covered, there can only be 21 million bitcoins in circulation due to the mining constraints. There are 7 billion people on this planet and as the adoption of Bitcoin as a global currency grows, there will be friction in the market caused due to growing demand and increasingly limited supply. This friction will lead to the rise in value of Bitcoin. It will also be amplified due to the fact that the popular strategy among many crypto-investors seems to be to "buy and hold". We will look at investing strategies in a later chapter.

2. **Mining difficulty**: Unlike fiat currencies which are minted by the national governments based on various monetary policies, cryptocurrencies are

mined by volunteers. Mining cryptocurrencies requires a lot of electrical and processing power. And the cost is not getting any cheaper. So, the inherent difficulty involved in creating a unit of cryptocurrency leads to a certain perceived value. This goes up as the mining difficulty increases. Basic economics states that the price of something that is rare and valuable will be high. Many cryptocurrencies use POW (Proof of Work) protocol while mining new coins and validating transactions. And the POW protocol rewards miners who have spent more time and effort solving harder problems. This is a fair way to incentivize the miners and also ensure that there is a direct correlation between the price of the cryptocurrency and mining difficulty. For more details on this, check out my book *"Blockchain:*

The Technology Revolution behind Bitcoin and Cryptocurrency" on Amazon.

3. **User Requirements**: If a cryptocurrency has no practical benefits to users, how is it any good? The cryptocurrency has to solve user's problems to be considered valuable. This is similar to how a company's stock value will plummet if it's not delivering any good quality products/services to its customers. In addition to being a means of value exchange, many cryptocurrencies offer distinctive solutions to domains like legal contracts, digital security, Internet of Things etc. This makes the investors fund the project and the customers register and use it.

4. **Public Opinion**: This is one of the most underrated causes of price surges for not only cryptocurrencies but any other publicly traded stock/commodity. Despite what we may believe, a majority of people think emotionally and take decisions based on their gut. The term "panic selling" is famous among traders and investors. Any major news like a security breach or a market crisis will make the value drop. This happened in Feb 2014 when Mt.Gox, the most famous crypto-exchange at that time filed for bankruptcy as a result of cyber-attacks. When it comes to Bitcoin, a lot of people believe that the independent decentralized nature of currency will be more beneficial since it is less prone to corruption, fraud and manipulation by central banks and governments. The other side of the coin (no pun

intended) is that there are also a lot of people who believe that Bitcoin is a currency used mostly by drug-dealers and criminals online. Nevertheless, the fact of the matter is that cryptocurrencies are blowing up globally and more people are becoming aware of the current crypto landscape and what it has to offer.

5. **Media & Law:** The price of a cryptocurrency can rise or fall depending on how the media portrays it to the public. There is always the possibility of getting blindsided by manipulative media. A few corporations or individuals who hold vested interest in a cryptocurrency can publicize its ICO (Initial Coin Offering) to bloat up its price in the market. This is why you should always do proper market research and look into a

wide variety of sources including reddit forums, quora answers, facebook groups, google news/trends and multiple news and publishing articles. If you're tech-savvy, I would also advise you to delve into the source code and developer updates. Legal notices, Nation-wide bans and anti-cryptocurrency policies have also been observed in the recent past. Countries like China, Vietnam and Russia are active in their protest against public usage of bitcoin. This caused a temporary dip in the price of bitcoin but soon bounced back up to an all-time high. Meanwhile, many countries like Canada, UK, Australia are embracing the crypto-revolution and have provided infrastructure and policy support to the cryptocurrency communities. Some of them even have Bitcoin ATMs available across various cities.

6. **Investors**: The fact that a cryptocurrency startup has received funding from a good investor can boost its coin price in the market. Investments are generally considered signs of trust. So, when a good/popular investor decides to put in capital for growing a cryptocurrency, a large portion of people decide to place their bets on it as well. Some malicious investors can also try to buy a large portion of the coins, inflate the price with press-releases or promotions and then sell them off quickly without any real progress. This is also referred to as the *pump and dump* strategy. The investors thus have a considerably high impact on the pricing of cryptocurrencies (especially altcoins with lower market caps).

7. **Market dilution**: With more than 1000 cryptocurrencies currently in the market and more coming in every year, the market sure has gotten crowded with so many alternatives. Even if an innovative solution is offered by a brand-new cryptocurrency in the market, it doesn't take too long before a competitor opens shop with lesser token price and upgraded capabilities. This causes frequent and unexpected spikes in the prices of cryptocurrencies. Bitcoin, though, is considered a reserve cryptocurrency since it has the highest market cap and largest user-base, owing to its first mover advantage. Fluctuation in bitcoin price usually causes a ripple effect and creates a fluctuation in prices of other cryptocurrencies as well.

Chapter-4: Your First Crypto Investment

Now that we know what cryptocurrencies are, how they work and how to buy and store them securely, it is time to make our first crypto-investment. If you're a beginner to cryptoinvesting, just follow the 5-step process described here. And don't skip any steps in haste or put in more than $100 maximum for your first couple of purchases.

Step-1: Sign up for a Wallet

A wallet, as we've covered in the previous chapter, is the first and foremost thing that you will need before you start investing in cryptocurrencies. The most famous and probably the best wallet for beginners currently in the market is Coinbase. It is an online platform where you can buy and hold cryptocurrencies. You can use regular fiat currencies like USD ($), GBP (£) to purchase cryptocurrencies like Bitcoin, Ethereum, Litecoin etc. All you need to do is register with your e-mail and provide a proof of identification. After that, you can transfer money from your bank account via Credit card, Debit card etc. You can use the link below to register and get $10 worth of Bitcoin for FREE in your wallet for future trades.

www.coinbase.com/join/598b36cb68284c0125fa0aea

Although Coinbase is a great platform, it is best for purchasing the most famous cryptocurrencies like Bitcoin, Ethereum, Litecoin etc. To buy lesser known cryptocurrencies, you have to use an exchange like Poloniex or GDAX (step-3). If this is the case, you can still use Coinbase to purchase some reserve cryptocurrency like Bitcoin and trade it with the lesser known coins on an exchange. Here is what the Coinbase interface looks like.

Coinbase Interface

While signing up for Coinbase, make sure to follow all the required steps and provide all the necessary details. You can register as an individual or a business organization. You can initially choose to register as an Individual. And after that, you need to provide your phone number and a valid ID (driver's license, passport etc.). Once you provide these, it will take a few minutes for Coinbase to verify your credentials. After that, you can choose a payment method to transfer funds from your bank account to your Coinbase wallet. Once this is done, you will be taken to the main Coinbase interface to proceed further.

Step-2: Get some coins in your Wallet

Once you finish the registration process, you will be able to login to your Coinbase account and see your crypto portfolio. Of course, if you're a beginner, you won't have any coins in your portfolio. So, you need to select the Buy/Sell option and choose your payment method. You have two options here. One is to use your credit/debit card and the other is to input your bank account details and directly transfer funds to Coinbase. The credit/debit card option will impose a limit on daily fund transfer to your coinbase account whereas the bank account option has no such limits. However, as you keep transferring more money into your coinbase wallet, the limit will gradually decrease so that you can transfer more.

Once you've entered the payment details, you can select the cryptocurrency and the amount of coins you want to purchase. There will be a tiny exchange fee charged by coinbase on the total amount you want to buy with. And this depends on your country and the currency you're using to buy the cryptocurrency with.

Once your purchase is confirmed, you will get the coins into your coinbase wallet. Now, Coinbase supports multiple wallets for multiple cryptocurrencies. So, your portfolio will show you separate wallets for bitcoin, ethereum, litecoin and the total amount of each cryptocurrency in those wallets. This makes it easier for you to transfer coins to a cryptoexchange and buy other cryptocurrencies with them.

Step-3: Move coins from Wallet to Exchange

Once you have actually put some money into your coinbase wallet, you will need to send it to a cryptoexchange for trading and investing in other cryptocurrencies. For this, you will need to register with a Cryptoexchange like GDAX, Poloniex, Bittrex etc. Refer to the section on Cryptocurrency Exchanges in the previous chapter to decide which one suits you best. Once you register to the cryptoexchange, go to the

"Send/Request" interface in Coinbase and enter the details like your email-address (registered with the exchange), the amount and cryptocurrency you want to transfer. You can choose from various wallets in your coinbase portfolio while sending coins to the exchange. If you choose GDAX, you will have easier time with this because it is integrated with Coinbase.

Step-4: Choose a Cryptocurrency to Buy

For the majority of people, the first trade either makes them or breaks them. So, it is very important for you to get comfortable with the process and accept the volatility of the market instead of being afraid of it.

The detailed methodology for picking a profitable cryptocurrency to invest in will be discussed in the upcoming chapters. But that's for building a long-term crypto portfolio. For your first investment, you don't have to be so aggressive in your picking criteria. This step is essentially just to get you going with the process of buying and selling. Having said that, here are some of the things to keep in mind while choosing the first test currency.

Don't choose something that is currently riding a bull wave. It shouldn't have a huge price increase in the very recent past. Login to the cryptoexchange and check the price charts. Click on the "Change" column in the Price Charts table and it should show you a list of cryptocurrencies in descending order of positive price change. So, the currencies in the top of the list have undergone massive increase in the price. They don't make good first investments because the hype wave will fall eventually and you will lose money. You want to choose a cryptocurrency that is priced low but has high potential in the near future. So, the price graph of the cryptocurrency should be flat currently but have high peaks in the past. Or maybe the graph is flat and you get some sort of intelligence from other trading groups or analysts or YouTube channels that it's going to blow up. In any case, the biggest criterion is that the price graph should be relatively flat and it should have a high future potential. You can even buy a coin whose price is going up provided it's in the early stages i.e., in the beginning phase of the wave. And also, it helps if the coin price is low – perhaps in the $1 to $10 range as opposed to Bitcoin which is worth tens of thousands of dollars for one coin. The reason for this is that you can experiment more with lower priced coins initially. The more bets you make, the higher your chance of winning and the easier it will be for you to get acquainted with the whole process.

Step-5: Place the Buy Order

After selecting your initial cryptocurrency to invest in, you need to place a buy order for it. A buy order consists of the amount you want to buy and the price you want to buy at. When the market price of the currency matches your estimate, the order is placed and the coins are transferred to your wallet. So, if the price chart of the currency indicates a dip in value, you can put in a price lower than the current market price and as soon as that is reached, you will have made a purchase.

To place a buy order in GDAX, go to the extreme left and select the "LIMIT" tab. Select "BUY" and enter the details. Most often, buy orders are placed with the reserve cryptocurrency (like Bitcoin, Ethereum etc.) that you have in your cryptoexchange. So, if you want to place a higher buy order, you need to transfer more coins from your wallet. Once you place your order, you can view it or cancel it in the "OPEN ORDERS" section.

Step-6: Place the Sell Order

This is pretty straightforward. When the market price of your currency reaches a desirable level, you can place a sell order to capture the profits. Just select the cryptocurrency, go to the "SELL" section (this will be adjacent to the "BUY" section) and enter the amount you want to sell and the price you want to sell at. You can compare your selling price with the "Highest Bid" value to get a sense of how likely it is to make the sale. After that, just click on "Sell" and it will be updated in the "OPEN ORDERS" section until it's fulfilled. Easy Peasy!

Chatper-5: How to Conduct Market Research

There are many online platforms like YouTube channels, blogs, forums, facebook groups, mailing lists etc. that you can go to for researching about the best cryptocurrency to invest in. But the underlying principle for any research methodology or technique is – KISS. It stands for Keep It Simple, Stupid. Time and again, the investing gurus and wall street giants have said that the simple solution is most often the best solution.

The first step in your research process is to go through the list at CoinMarketCap and pick a few interesting cryptocurrencies. Then, you're going to Google them and check if any of them have had a successful ICO in the past. ICO stands for Initial Coin Offering and is basically the launch of a new cryptocurrency. A successful ICO will attract a lot of attention from investors, users, media and will raise a lot of funds for the cryptocurrency project to move forward. So, that should be your first sign of a good coin to invest in.

Other than that, here are 4 criteria you can use to make sure that you pick a winning cryptocurrency for your portfolio in the long term.

Criteria #1: Is the current value of the coin in your "comfort zone" range? Another way to put it is, are you OK with buying the cryptocurrency this moment given that it may have dropped very low in the recent past or might do so in the near future? Is the current coin price close to the all-time low? If not then it's alright if you choose not to invest. We want to make sure that there are no "buy walls" that stop us from applying a long-term investment strategy. If you're not comfortable with the initial buy-in price, either you will not be able to hold it for long or you'll feel really bad if the coin price plummets. So, only buy coins at a price you're absolutely comfortable with.

Criteria #2: Are any innovations or new technologies going to be built on top of the cryptocurrency platform? You can search on

Twitter, YouTube, Forums, Google News for any related research papers, publications, blog posts or news articles for this. The essential idea is that piggybacking on a breakthrough innovation will boost the coin price sooner or later. And if a new technology startup based on the cryptocurrency gets funded by a Venture Capital firm, that is almost a sure shot way of reaping huge profits on your initial investment. So, if you notice any such news, place your bets as soon as possible before the majority get on it and inflate the prices.

Criteria #3: Is there a community of like-minded people who depend on the cryptocurrency or are incentivized to grow it? From an investment perspective, one of the biggest factors to consider is trust. And nothing gives you more trust in a coin than support from a solid community with common goals and interests. Cryptocurrencies like STEEM, Stratis, Ripple have thrived in the recent past as a result of having strong community support.

Criteria #4: How unique is the technology behind the cryptocurrency? If it's relatively simple to reproduce, the cryptocurrency would face massive competition in the market from alternative coins that offer better features. So, you have to research about the IP (Intellectual Property) behind the cryptocurrency and the replication difficulty. If it has a huge user base, ask yourself "What can make the users shift to an alternative?". The more unique the cryptocurrency, the deeper it can penetrate into the market.

These are the four top criteria I use to filter through the various options available and find ones that can benefit me in the long term. You can also find profitable investments by observing the graphs in a CryptoExchange. Although Coinbase and CoinMarketCap are good places to start from, if you're interested in digging deeper and want to pick up on more subtle market trends, GDAX is the place to go to. GDAX (Global Digital Asset Exchange) is a trading platform for advanced Coinbase users. They are mutually compatible so you can use the same login credentials on GDAX as Coinbase and also easily transfer cryptoassets between them.

Upgrading to GDAX will give you a lot of benefits including a lower transaction fee on trades and other additional features like real-time pricing data, simple visualizations and charts etc.

Here are some major features of GDAX that will help you identify profitable coins in the cryptomarket.

1. **Price Chart:** This is the most famous and most frequently used chart of GDAX. It shows the pricing and volume data of the cryptocurrency over time. The candlesticks in the chart show the open point and close point of the particular time period.

2. **Depth Chart:** Present just below the Price Chart, the Depth Chart (figure 2. below) will help you identify the demand and supply of the cryptocurrency. The chart consists of essentially two graphs. One for the BIDs (Buy orders) and one for the ASKs (Sell orders). In the depth chart, the green portion (left side) indicates the buy orders a.k.a demand and the red portion (right side) indicates the sell orders a.k.a supply. For example, you can select a point on the ASK graph and know how many units you can sell (cumulatively) at that particular price point.

Depth Chart

3. **Order Book:** This is present on the left side of the price chart. It's like a live counter, showing all the current open orders on the GDAX platform. You can click on an order and choose to buy/sell the same amount for your own order. And this

new order will be updated in real time for you to see on the counter.

4. **Trade History:** This is pretty straight forward. It's basically a view just like the *Order Book* but on the right side of the price chart. It shows a list of all the fulfilled orders on the platform. Everything here is updated in real time so you can monitor it to get an insight on the market trend.

If you have any prior knowledge on stock trading or other financial strategies or pattern analysis, GDAX is the best tool you can use for identifying opportunities. For a full-length detailed guide on how to make profits by trading cryptocurrencies, check out my best-selling book *"Cryptocurrency Trading"* on Amazon. Also, if you want to keep track of cryptocurrencies and where they're trading at, I would recommend a mobile app called Blockfolio (www.blockfolio.com). You can view your whole portfolio at once on your mobile which is very convenient. They also offer some management tools and price alerts.

Investing in Altcoins

Altcoins, as you must already be aware of by now, are cryptocurrencies that are not Bitcoin. As it happens, Bitcoin currently holds the lion's share of the crypto market. For many beginners, it may be overpriced or overwhelming. For such folks, there are a variety of altcoins available in the market that cost only a fraction of what Bitcoin costs.

If you're interested in investing in an altcoin, you must be cautious of the hype that goes around before it's ICO (Initial Coin Offering). Most altcoins don't live up to the hype in the long run. So here are some tips to keep in mind before you put your money into an altcoin.

Tip #1: Check BTC correlations

Many altcoins have buy/sell trends that are directly affected by Bitcoin's pricing. When Bitcoin's value rises, there is generally a plunge in altcoin's value and vice versa. So, you must have a knowledge of Bitcoin's recent performance as well as a prediction of its future before investing in an altcoin. If you want to minimize risk, you should find an altcoin that has a decently high Bitcoin reserve.

Tip #2: Check backing and user-base

This goes without saying. You need to research about the goals, team, features provided by the altcoin. Many altcoins have a cult-like following that you can capitalize on. For example, Dogecoin, which is a cryptocurrency that is literally inspired from an internet meme of a dog, has gone from a market cap of $60 million in 2014 to $580 million in 2017. And apparently a Dogecoin made out of gold is being sent to the moon in 2019!

Tip #3: Diversify your portfolio

Diversification is one of the best ways to minimize risk as an altcoin-investor. You should hold a reserve amount in stable altcoins that have a relatively decent future in terms of support and growth. Risks with ICOs and day trading should be done with a minor portion of your money that doesn't affect the rest of your portfolio.

Here are some more questions you should ask yourself before investing into a selected altcoin.
- What core problem is the altcoin attempting to solve and how big is it?
- Is there a solid marketing strategy for the altcoin to reach target users?
- **Social Proof**: Are any other investors or VCs interested in funding the cryptocurrency? What are the tech moguls saying about it?

- **Buzz**: Is there sufficient positive news coverage? How many hardcore followers does the altcoin have on social-media?
- Is there a possible scenario for market manipulation in the altcoin's future? How dependent is it on the founders and core investors?
- What has the altcoin's performance been in the past?

Chatper-6: Essential Tips & Strategies

Most crypto-enthusiasts and traders just go to an exchange and buy whatever seems to be going up in price. And when the price starts going down, they panic and sell it off in a quick attempt to make a buck. This is an impulse-driven strategy that is not sustainable in the long-term. Everyday, hundreds and thousands of people (if not millions) lose money on stock and crypto exchanges because they lack the essential knowledge of proper buy-in and sell-out strategies. In this chapter, we will be looking at some common investment strategies as well as some useful tips that can help you deal with the crypto market in a smooth and sane way.

Buying Strategies

There are two main strategies when it comes to cryptoinvesting. The short-term and the long-term. The short-term strategy usually has a lot of risks and frauds involved with it. But they are both viable methods for getting good ROIs if you know what you're doing.

Short-term buying: Pump and Dump

Yes, the phrase "pump and dump" does sound a bit sketchy. But it's actually a legit way of investing and reaping the profits. The basic idea is to identify any market news from forums, youtube etc. that is hyping up a certain cryptocurrency. Then, get in on that before the hype wave starts and ride it until the price starts dropping. You don't need to research on the possible impact the coin may have in the future or any such thing. Hype waves are real. They happen quite often in the market. And the short-term strategy is to identify them and ride them successfully. You can make great gains on a hot coin using this strategy.

The "pump" refers to the rise in coin value and the "dump" refers to the selling point. Many investors who hold significant share of a cryptocurrency try to promote it in whatever way possible to inflate the price. And once the price reaches a certain point, they start selling it like crazy. You can identify such kind of scenarios by observing the cryptocurrency community on Reddit, Youtube and forums. The secret to this strategy is to be alert and identify the coins that are blowing up.

Long-term buying: Buy and Hold

The *Buy and Hold* strategy is what seems to getting more popular among beginner crypto-traders and investors. As the name suggests, it involves buying a high-traffic or high-potential cryptocurrency like Bitcoin or Ethereum and holding it long-term (5 years) in order to reap the benefits later. It's a 'set it and forget it' type of situation. Once you hold the stock, you don't even check the news or get any updates regarding the price surges. This is because the *buy and hold* strategy requires you to be impervious to impulsive decision-making. On the off chance that the cryptocurrency you're holding is blowing up in price like crazy and you want to capture some of the profit, you may decide to sell some of your stock in installments. But make sure to hold the majority of it in your wallet for the long-term.

You need to pick a good entry-point to effectively capture the profit from this buy and hold strategy. For example, Ripple (XRP) went from $8 billion in December 2017 to nearly $130 billion in early January 2018. Even if you research Ripple and feel that it's a good long-term investment, buying the coins when the price is inflated is a bad idea. You need to deploy some patience and wait for the price to level down before holding it for the future. That's just common sense.

Keep in mind that proper market-research is very crucial for the long-term strategy. You need to gather enough domain knowledge to predict whether the cryptocurrency platform will be able to withstand any major technological, political, social changes for a long period of time. It helps if you have an affinity with the coin's community and core features.

One of the biggest hurdles to applying the buy and hold strategy is the temporary price surges. This is when you will be tempted to sell your coins off and make a profit. I've faced this before and I can say that it's hard to overcome because the market provides easy validation to your belief in the coin. Your conviction will be tested. That is when you have to go back to the market research you conducted and get clear on the reasons why holding the coin for the long-term will pay off.

Mix & Match: Playing the Market

This is a hybrid of the two strategies mentioned before. In this, you maintain a portfolio where some coins are held for the long-term while others are bought and sold quickly as per the market value a.k.a pump and dump. You will be monitoring the coin valuations regularly and making necessary updates to your crypto investments. Although it's an active process of hedging bets, you'll be minimizing the risk because you won't be dependent on any single strategy or coin. And even when your long-term coins are flat lining, you can still profit from the temporary market fluctuations.

Exit Strategies

This is one of the most important parts of cryptocurrency investing but unfortunately most people forget to take care of it. An exit strategy is a way of reaping the profits you made from your investments. Just holding on to your coins in the wallet isn't an exit strategy. What is the endpoint? How do you plan to benefit from the returns? Here are two main points you need to think about while creating an exit strategy.

1. **Purpose:** Why are you interested in cryptoinvesting in the first place? What do you need the profits for? Is it to pay off your debts? Is it for a retirement fund or mortgage? Or is it just to accumulate wealth/assets? No reason is wrong. But if you fail to be clear in it, you will spend too much time playing the market. This is a journey. There is a starting point and there is an ending point. You need to decide both or you will end up disoriented.

2. **Target Capital:** How much worth of cryptocurrency do you plan to hold that will achieve your purpose? Is it $100,00 or 1 million or 1 billion? Again, no price point is wrong. You just have to be clear about what you want. A friend of mine put in around $2000 into Bitcoin in early January of 2017. By the end of the year, he cashed out $34,000 to pay off his debts. People called him crazy for not holding on to his invaluable bitcoins. But what they failed to realize was that he was not a gambler. He knew when to quit. He made the profits he needed and had no regrets at all. When it comes to

investing, that is the right attitude to have.

Cashing Out Your Cryptocurrency

Once you make some profits with cryptoinvesting or trading on the exchange, you would naturally want to get some of it back into your crypto-wallet and eventually into your bank account. This process is fairly simple. For GDAX, just click on the "WITHDRAW" button on the left pane after logging in. Since GDAX is integrated with Coinbase, you can directly select the amount and your wallet and click on "Withdraw Funds". You can also withdraw funds to any other holding account. All you need is a Bitcoin Address and the two-factor authentication code that'll be sent to your mobile via SMS.

To withdraw funds from Poloniex, just select the "Balances" section or go to www.poloniex.com/balances. After this, go to Coinbase, copy the wallet address and enter it into Poloniex. Make sure that the cryptocurrency you want to withdraw matches the cryptocurrency stored in the coinbase wallet. Otherwise, you need to convert the cryptocurrency on your exchange accordingly.

There will be a daily withdrawal limit and also a withdrawal fee charged depending on your usage and choice of exchange.

Once you get the cryptocurrency into your coinbase wallet, suppose BTC wallet, you need to sell it and receive fiat currency in return. For this, you can setup a separate wallet for fiat currency (let's say USD) on Coinbase. And after you sell your BTC and receive USD in your USD wallet, you can select it and click on "Withdraw" button on top-right. If you've setup your payment method properly while registering for Coinbase, your USD will then be deposited into your bank account shortly.

Chatper-7: How to Profit from ICOs

In this chapter, we will be looking at what ICOs are, how they work, what benefits they offer to crypto investors and how you can find a profitable ICO in the market. Let's get started.

What is an ICO?

As you must've already been aware of by now, ICO is an acronym that stands for Initial Coin Offering. It's the crypto-equivalent of an IPO (Initial Public Offering) where a company goes public and releases its shares to be traded on stock exchanges like NASDAQ, NYSE etc. An ICO, however, is different in that it is used to raise capital for a cryptocurrency without having to deal with all the regulations and financial blabber of venture capitalists. It's a quick and smooth way for startups to receive crowdfunding in exchange for selling their crypto "tokens" to investors. These "tokens" can be bought by early supporters of the startup's cryptocurrency with legal tender or other famous cryptocurrencies like Bitcoin, Ethereum etc. When the startup finishes its goals/projects, these tokens will be converted into actual coins which will then supposedly be worth much more in value.

Advantages of investing in ICOs

1. **Lower Price Point:** The regular way of buying a cryptocurrency involves going to the exchange and getting the coins at the available market price. However, an ICO offers you the unique opportunity to buy coins at the pre-release price which is usually much lower than the eventual market price. So, you're essentially bagging the cryptocurrency before it's offered on the market.

2. **Very High ROI Potential:** Since you can purchase the crypto tokens for cheaper price, if the ICO succeeds and the project comes through, you will be in possession of coins that are exponentially more profitable. On average, if you diversify your ICOs enough, the chances of you making 10X to

20X returns are incredibly high. Typically, 1 or 2 out of your every 10 ICO investments will succeed and cover the losses in addition to bringing a huge ROI.

3. **Opportunity to Fund a Breakthrough:** This is one of the primary advantages of participating in an ICO. If you conduct proper research and have sufficient domain knowledge, you can identify winning startups that have the potential to revolutionize the industry and create billions of dollars in value. This is what happened with Ethereum back in 2014. For the "Smart Contracts" project, Ethereum launched a successful ICO with their "Ether" tokens, raising an initial capital of $18 million.

Today, the market cap of Ethereum is more than $100 billion.

Where to find good ICOs

Many times, you need to be part of a closely-knit community to get invited to an ICO. And the initial tokens will be available to only those members with an invite who show particular enthusiasm for the cryptocurrency and the project. So, it really helps if you have a network of friends/acquaintances who are involved in the cryptocurrency community. However, you can also take part in many public and semi-private ICOs if you know where to find them. Here are a few starting points to explore.

- Social Media: A lot of prominent cryptocurrency experts and journals have active Twitter accounts that you can follow to get notifications about latest ICOs, market fluctuations etc. Here are a few twitter handles for reference - @CharlieShrem, @VitalikButerin, @NicTrades.

    Apart from Twitter, there are also some great Facebook groups that you can join to connect with some really cool cryptotraders and investors. Check out the facebook group "Cryptocurrency Collectors Club".

- Google News: This is a great source for picking up on any public chatter for a big ICO or market shift. Google will crawl and select the best news articles, blogs and publications that you can quickly skim through to find interesting options.

- <u>Youtube:</u> There are a lot of youtube channels dedicated to the cryptocurrency market. You can pick and choose the people you most relate with. I'd recommend "Chris Dunn", "Ameer Rosic" and "DataDash".
- Websites like ICO Watch list, Best Coins, ICO Alert

How to buy ICO tokens

This depends on the ICO you're interested in. Most cryptocurrencies will let you sign up on their website and create an account. Once you enter the amount of ICO tokens you want to purchase, you will be given a wallet address that you can transfer bitcoins to. Just go back to your Coinbase wallet and enter the wallet address and the appropriate BTC amount. After the send is successful, it usually takes 15-30 minutes for you to receive the ICO tokens on your new cryptocurrency account. Always make sure to send the coins directly from your wallet to the ICO's wallet and not via an exchange.

So, there you have it. In this chapter, you've learnt what ICOs are, how they differ from regular IPOs, why ICOs are great opportunities for making profitable crypto investments, how to find good ICOs and how to buy the ICO tokens. In the next chapter, we will be looking at what the future of cryptocurrencies may look like and how you can adapt to the changing market as a crypto investor.

Chatper-8: Future of Cryptocurrencies

Cryptocurrencies have a smaller user base compared to regular fiat currencies. But as technology improves and more infrastructure and awareness are created around the world, the impact of cryptocurrencies is inevitable and immense.

Venture Capitalists have invested more than 1 Billion dollars into the blockchain technology itself. This is an indication of the scope of development that is bound to occur in this field in the upcoming future. Below is a graph showing the increase in number of user-wallets of bitcoin's blockchain.

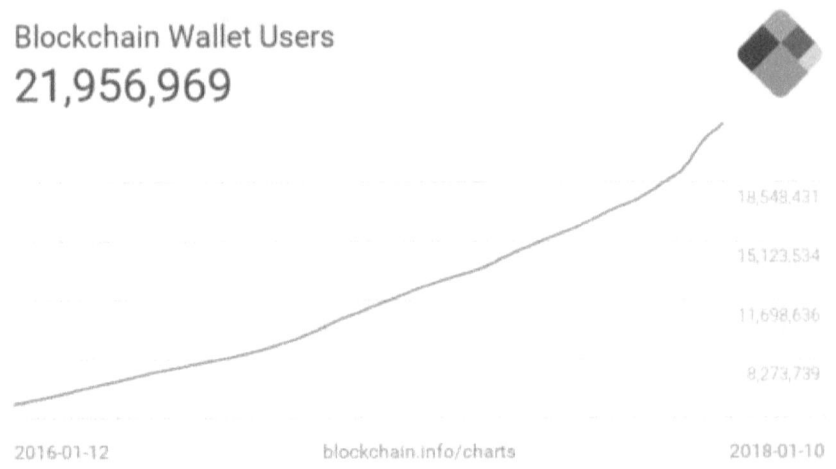

Is it all just a big bubble?

Many people ask this question when they see the market prices plunge up/down. One of the biggest arguments people make in this regard is, "Well, if it's decentralized, who's going to back it up?" There is no central authority backing up the system. So, it is easy to fall into the trap of thinking that cryptocurrencies are just treading on thin ice and have no solid ground to stand on. But this couldn't be farther from the fact. What gives, say, Bitcoin, its value is its huge user base and widespread acceptance. If you think about it, that's what gives anything value – Public acceptance. Not centralized government backing. If you take a commodity like an Apple iPhone and ask the question "Why is it worth what it's worth?" the answer will be the same. IPhones are not backed by the government the way fiat currencies are. They are just products made by a company that people have come to assign great value to, over time. So, cryptocurrencies get their value the same way an iPhone gets its value. Public acceptance. The more they're used by the people, the more they're worth.

With cryptocurrencies, it is almost certain at this point that the total market cap will reach $1Trillion within the next 5 years. We are currently at a total of around $584 Billion. With the amount of progress being made in this field, even with a temporary value-drop or a bubble-pop, the rise of cryptocurrencies and blockchain technology is inevitable. So, brace yourselves for what is to come. Having said that, if you follow some of the tips & strategies mentioned in previous chapters, diversify your portfolio and use common sense, you will be sure to have a long and prosperous journey.

There are more and more cryptocurrencies coming into the market every month. As time goes on, we will see a range of cryptocurrencies offering different services for users. Bitcoin being the first one out there, will have an initial head start in terms of user adoption. But with all the latest innovations and the attention being paid to this space, it is difficult to predict whether bitcoin will be overtaken by other cryptocurrencies or not. Bitcoin currently occupies nearly 50% of the total market share of cryptocurrencies. Given the rising popularity of new cryptocurrencies, this situation may eventually change. But having been first to the market and being the reserve cryptocurrency to almost all other coins, Bitcoin will most likely hold the #1 position in the upcoming future.

The advent of new cryptocurrencies will be paralleled by an emergence of new crypto-exchanges. So, it will get easier for merchants and buyers to transfer the money and convert between two cryptocurrencies.

Having said this, I think we need to look at both sides of the coin (no pun intended). One of the biggest problems facing the mass adoption of cryptocurrencies is their lack of scalability. Bitcoin, for example, has had a huge growth in the number of transactions being carried out. The graph below, sourced from Wikipedia, shows how the number of transactions has been growing every year. But here's the catch – The block-size in Bitcoin is limited to 1MB. So, any blocks bigger than this are rejected by the network. This has resulted in limiting the number of transactions per second that can be processed by the network to three. To counter this limit, bitcoin miners have opted to upgrade the software so that the block-size can be increased to 2MB. This will increase the transaction fee but reduce the congestion in the network.

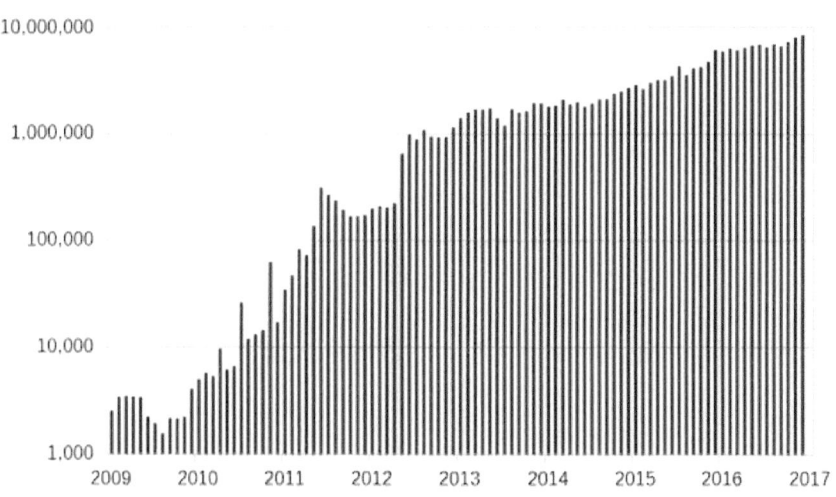

Bitcoin also had a bear market crash in the past (July 2017) where it's value dropped by around

20% in a 7-day period. Although the value is back up again, it would be foolish to believe that the cryptocurrency market is not volatile. It is highly advised for anyone interested in investing into cryptocurrencies or anyone that has already done so, to follow the latest updates and stay informed.

The Changing Landscape of Global Finance

With features like lower latency of transactions and reduced transaction fee, cryptocurrencies (especially bitcoin) have a potential for disrupting the e-commerce industry as well. The current online payment methods that users have to rely on for purchasing stuff online have lousy user experience, charge more per transaction and take longer to process payments. This gives cryptocurrencies like Bitcoin an opportunity to replace the traditional methods and create positive impact.

Due to its decentralized nature, Bitcoin has been facing restricted compliance from the banks and financial organizations. Its value dropped quite a bit when China banned Bitcoin from being used within its borders. But with blockchain, it's a different story. Financial institutions are showing positive response to the possibility of embracing the public ledger system. The reason for this seems to be the increase in operational efficiency created by using the blockchain technology.

Cryptocurrencies also seem to be advantageous for third-world countries that have under-developed financial infrastructure. These countries can bypass the need for spending a lot of tax money into public banks, mints and other regulatory financial organizations by directly adopting global cryptocurrencies like Bitcoin. What we're looking at is actually the possibility of unifying the world's currencies.

There are a lot of experiments being conducted in this space and despite all the hype, cryptocurrencies are still in their early stages. So, there is absolutely no need for you to feel like you're missing out on the party. Cryptocurrencies and blockchain have the potential to change not only the payment industry but also the way business is done. With widespread decentralized distributed digital currencies, there would be no need for separate national fiat currencies. All countries around the world could fall back on a single platform of value exchange. If it happens, this will be a landmark achievement in the history of human progress. Although we have a long way to go before achieving that stage, it is quite obvious that the future of cryptocurrencies is very bright indeed.

A few final words

Congratulations! You've made it to the end. Hopefully, it's been a fun and educational experience. I've certainly had a blast preparing this book for you. And once again, I want to express my deepest gratitude to you for having given me your time and attention. I hope you found great value worth your investment. If you did, I want you to just do this ONE thing for me.

Please leave an honest review on Amazon at the link below. That is the only way for me to get your feedback and improve my craft. Thanks a ton!

www.bookstuff.in/cryptoinvesting-review

More from the author

Blockchain: The Technology Revolution behind Bitcoin and Cryptocurrency

Cryptocurrency Trading: How to Make Money by Trading Bitcoin and other Cryptocurrency

Bitcoin: The Digital Gold

Cryptocurrency: The Essential Guide to understanding Bitcoin, Blockchain & More

www.ingramcontent.com/pod-product-compliance
Lightning Source LLC
Chambersburg PA
CBHW020423220526
45464CB00002B/539